SUPERHEROES

FAITH OUT LOUD

DISCIPLESHIP MINISTRY TEAM
MINISTRY COUNCIL
CUMBERLAND PRESBYTERIAN CHURCH

SEPTEMBER 2015

8207 TRADITIONAL PLACE
CORDOVA (MEMPHIS), TENNESSEE 38016

Funded, in part, by your contributions to Our United Outreach.

First Edition 2015

Published by The Discipleship Ministry Team, CPC
Memphis, Tennessee

ISBN-13: 978-0692536995
ISBN-10: 069253699X

We want to hear from you.
Please send your comments about this curriculum to
the Discipleship Ministry Team at faithoutloud@cumberland.org

OUR UNITED OUTREACH
Made Possible In Part By Your Tithe To Our United Outreach

FAITH OUT LOUD

BATMAN, PUNISHER, AND THE PURSUIT OF VENGEANCE

BY JIMMY BYRD and ANDY McCLUNG

SCRIPTURE
LEVITICUS 19:18, DEUTERONOMY 3:35,
ROMANS 12:19, MATTHEW 5:43-44

THEME
Both good guys and bad guys can be motivated by vengeance, but Christians are called to handle vengeance altogether differently.

CONECTING TO YOUR STUDENTS

Teens know just how hard it is to be good when so many forces tempt them to be bad. They, like most people in our society, are great at rationalizing and justifying sinful behavior. "It's okay because we're in love." "It's not right for them to have so much when I have so little, so it's okay to take this." "It's just a little white lie." Rationalizing sinful behavior too often, though, hampers the ability to recognize certain behaviors as sinful.

From every medium of entertainment to rivalries between sports teams, vengeance is constantly glorified and defended by culture. It's also encouraged by sinful human nature. It's one of the hardest temptations to resist, possibly because it feels like the most natural thing in the world.

But for Christ's sake, for our own sake, and for the sake of others, we are called to resist the temptation of vengeance.

An entire Faith Out Loud lesson deals with "Revenge vs Forgiveness."
Find it in 2013's Volume 3, Quarter 1."

EXPLAINING THE TOPIC

Vengeance is a constant theme in superhero stories, pursued by both heroes and villains. For this lesson, we'll focus on four characters.

Vengeance—violent revenge, or the desire for revenge.

Batman first appeared in Detective Comics #27 in 1939, but his origin story was told later. Bruce Wayne, the beloved only child of ridiculously rich parents, had a life of wealth, luxury, and leisure all laid out for him. While still a child, Bruce witnessed his parents senselessly murdered during a mugging in an alley. The loss of his parents was devastating, of course. Their deaths, however, didn't change Bruce's future. He still had a life of wealth, luxury, and leisure all laid out for him. But instead of taking solace in that fact and embracing a life of ease, he swore vengeance upon not just the murderous mugger, but on all criminals. Using his fortune and leisure time, Bruce worked ridiculously hard to learn hand-to-hand combat skills, parkour-like urban movement, and how to solve crimes. He also designed and built a bunch of vehicles, weapons, tools, and costumes to help him seek vengeance and keep the innocent from experiencing a loss like his.

While Batman terrorizes and beats up criminals, he almost never kills them. There are a few exceptions, but none are outright murder. It's important to note that while driven by vengeance Batman also protects the innocent, sometimes even letting criminals get away in favor of saving bystanders. So his thirst for vengeance is tempered by a desire to do good.

The Joker, a supervillain who first appeared in Batman #1 in 1940, enjoys killing. He has no problem victimizing anyone to reach his own goals or just to have some fun. His motive, besides being insane, is vengeance. Joker's origin has been changed over the decades, but one has him as a normal criminal who became hideously disfigured when Batman knocked him into a vat of acid during a fight. In that story, Joker's motivation for crime and chaos is vengeance against Batman. Another origin story has Joker as a failed comedian who only turns to crime to feed his family. He ends up losing everything. His response is to go completely insane and take vengeance on the society that forced him to choose between crime and starvation.

Superman's arch-enemy, Lex Luthor, who first appeared in Action Comics #23 in 1940, was originally portrayed as a brilliant and megalomaniacal villain who wants to take over the world. He's so smart and resourceful, the only thing that can stop him is Superman. And Superman does stop him, repeatedly. In a 1960 story, though, we learn that Luthor and Superman were childhood friends. Superman saved Luthor's

The Punisher, a.k.a Frank Castle, is all about vengeance. He first appeared in Amazing Spider-Man #129 in 1974. He was a war veteran who, on a picnic with his family, stumbled upon a mafia execution in progress. The criminals shot the entire family to prevent witnesses. Frank alone survived and swore vengeance on all criminals, using his combat skills to wage war on crime. How's this different from Batman? Well, Frank doesn't have a secret identity, he doesn't wear a mask or costume (just a white skull on a black shirt), and without concern for collateral damage, his method of stopping crime is killing the criminals. He doesn't have to catch them red-handed, either. Punisher's methods often bring him into conflict with characters who are opposed to killing, like Spider-Man and Daredevil. Frank isn't interested in helping good people, only punishing the bad. And he's very good at doing just that. The Punisher, then, isn't quite a good guy, because he's a ruthless killer. But he's not quite a bad guy either, because he only kills criminals. He's an antihero, driven by vengeance. He's a popular character, possibly because many people harmed by criminals wish they could do what he does.

> Antihero—a protagonist who lacks the attributes that make a
> heroic figure, such as nobility of mind and spirit.

So, Batman seeks vengeance, but he doesn't kill and he protects innocents and victims. His motivation is equal parts vengeance and preventing criminals from harming new victims. According to culture, that makes him a good guy. The Joker and Lex Luthor lie, steal, cheat, and kill to get what they want. They're driven by vengeance and don't care who they hurt to achieve it. According to culture, that makes them bad guys. The Punisher only kills criminals. He steals, but only from bad guys and only to finance his war on crime. He doesn't kill criminals to prevent more crimes, though, but to punish them. According to culture, that makes him mostly a good guy.

THEOLOGICAL UNDERPINNINGS

Culture doesn't always reflect what God says is right and good. Culture says, in many various ways, "Seek vengeance against those who hurt you." God says, "You shall not take vengeance or bear a grudge against any of your people" (Leviticus 19:18), "Vengeance is mine" (Deuteronomy 3:35), and "never avenge yourselves" (Romans 12:19).

God designed us. God made us. God became one of us in Jesus. God knows us. God knows that our being focused on vengeance means we are dwelling on past injuries. Such dwelling on the negative past keeps us from moving toward a positive future, spiritually and emotionally. God knows that when we seek vengeance, we want so badly to see someone suffer like ourselves, we'll probably hurt people who had nothing to do with our injuries. This is especially true when we seek vengeance against a system that hurt us; we come to believe that anyone associated with that system is responsible for our pain. God knows we can make mistakes like blaming the wrong person and hurting an innocent person, thereby harming not only our victims, but spiritually harming ourselves as well.

God forbids vengeance because God knows that as soon as our hearts turn toward it, we cease seeing the target of our vengeance as another human being, created and loved by God. Instead, we see them as dehumanized objects. God created humankind in God's own image (Confession of Faith 1.11). When we objectify others, we're not seeing God in them.

When we seek vengeance, we are not honoring God or being Christ-like. And that's probably exactly why culture and our own sinful nature push us toward vengeance so readily and persistently.

APPLYING THE LESSON TO YOUR OWN LIFE

In entertainment, how often do you cheer for a character who is seeking vengeance? When you think about criminals and the justice system in the real world, do you think more about punishing perpetrators or protecting their potential future victims? Why?

What's the worst thing you've ever done to somebody? Did they seek vengeance? If so, did their seeking vengeance accomplish something positive, or perpetuate something negative?

What's the worst thing anybody has ever done to you? Did you seek vengeance? If so, did seeking vengeance accomplish something positive, or perpetuate something negative?

When we sin, we offend God. God doesn't seek vengeance for those offenses because God knows vengeance moves us away from God. Instead, God treats us with grace (giving us good things we don't deserve) and mercy (not giving us bad things we do deserve). Does vengeance draw us closer to others? Or does it move us away from our fellow humans who are created and loved by God?

BATMAN, PUNISHER, AND THE PURSUIT OF VENGEANCE

SCRIPTURE
LEVITICUS 19:18, DEUTERONOMY 3:35,
ROMANS 12:19, MATTHEW 5:43-44

LEADER PREP

LEADER PREP
To make things fun for this 6 week Superheroes study, you may want to decorate your classroom with a superhero theme. You can find all kinds of superhero decorations at a party supply store.

RESOURCE LIST
• Blank sheets of paper

• Colored pencils or markers

• Two pieces of newsprint or a dry erase board

• Old Suitcase

GET STARTED

INSTRUCTIONS
Say: "In pop culture today, we are bombarded with superheroes—The Avengers, Batman, Superman, Wonder Woman, Daredevil, Green Arrow, and The Flash—are a few that are currently featured in movies and TV shows."

OPTION #1: Since this is the first lesson in the Super Heroes series, have the students name and talk about their favorite superhero.
   • Why do they like this particular superhero?
   • What special powers, if any, does this superhero have?
   • What motivates this super hero do what they do?

Make sure each student gets enough time to describe their favorite super hero. Some students may not have a favorite, they may like more than one, or they may not like super heroes at all. (If a student does not have a favorite super hero, maybe ask them who they consider to be a hero in their life.)

OPTION #2: Give each student a piece of blank paper and something to draw with. Have them draw themselves as a super hero. They need to design their own costume, their own special powers, and come up with a really cool name. After everyone is finished, have them share with the rest of the group.

LISTEN UP

LISTEN UP (15 minutes)
The two characters at the center of this lesson are Batman and Punisher. Both are considered to be "good guys," but they both have baggage that affects how they pursue criminals.

Most students will be familiar with Batman but maybe not as familiar with Punisher. Refer back to the descriptions of Batman and Punisher from earlier in the lesson. You may need to read the descriptions to the students. If you have a laptop, tablet, or phone you can google the images of each one.

Put up two pieces of newsprint on the wall, or make two columns on a dry erase board. On one, write "How are Batman and Punisher similar". On the other write "How are Batman and Punisher different?" Have the students list answers for each category.

Ask: What motivates Batman and Punisher?
Answer: Vengeance, anger, revenge, both lost their families to violence.

Say: The Joker and Lex Luthor are two good examples of villains that glorify committing acts of violence. They both take out vengeance on society because of how they were wronged in the past. Because of their anger, they feel that everyone should suffer.

DISCUSSION QUESTIONS

Ask: Where do you draw the line between Batman and the Punisher, and the Joker and Lex Luthor? Let students debate that.

It is good that Batman and the Punisher want to stop the bad guys. The way they are doing it though, especially the Punisher, goes against biblical teaching.

Pick three students to each read the following passage.
Passage one: Leviticus 19:18 "You shall not take vengeance or bear a grudge against any of your people."
Passage two: Deuteronomy 3:35 "Vengeance is mine"
Passage three: Romans 12:19 "never avenge yourselves"

Ask: According to these scriptures, who has the authority for vengeance?
Answer: God

Ask: How come God gets to take vengeance but not us?
Answer: God is all powerful and all knowing. God is the ultimate judge of right and wrong. God is protecting us from making bad decisions.

Say: There are many stories where a central character is out for vengeance because someone has hurt them. Many times at the end of the story, after they have dished out their vengeance or revenge, they feel empty and lost because they have spent so much time and energy on getting back at that person.

Ask: Is vengeance the best way to get back at someone who has hurt us? Should we get back at someone who has hurt us? What should we do?

Have someone read Matthew 5:43-44. "You have heard that it was said, 'You shall love your neighbor and hate your enemy.' But I say to you, Love your enemies and pray for those who persecute you," (NRSV)

As of the time of writing this lesson, the riots in Baltimore, Maryland are taking place. This is an example being played out of how vengeance can lead to acts of violence and destruction. This might be a good example to use with the students for a discussion on appropriate ways to respond to feelings and allegations of injustice. Regardless of that incident, there have been ongoing feelings of injustice for many years, and this has stirred up a lot of emotions especially frustration and anger.

NOW WHAT

NOW WHAT? (10-15 minutes)

Say: Everyone has been hurt by someone and has been hurt by life in general. No matter how young or how old we are, we all get hurt. Sometimes it's a hurt that quickly goes away. Sometimes it takes a long time for it to go away. Sometimes the hurt never goes away.

Some of the students in your class may be experiencing some serious hurt and pain. Be aware of this, and if there is a situation where a student has been abused, it must be reported.

Say: We all carry around baggage. Some of the baggage isn't so heavy, but some of it is unbearable and weighs us down. Baggage can cause us to live in the past instead of in the now. Wouldn't it be great to get rid of some of that baggage?

Have the students list the baggage they are carrying around that they would like to give to God. For some it may be one thing, for others it may be a whole list. This is private, so no one should look at what another person has written down. Take a suitcase (an old one would be great), open it, and place it in the center of the room. After assuring the students that no one will be seeing these lists, have the students place their baggage lists in the suitcase. When all have finished placing them in the suitcase, close it. Pray over the "baggage," and ask God to help the students to be able to give that hurt to God and to allow God to find ways for them to deal with it other than vengeance. Afterwards you can throw away or shred the lists, or if it's an old suitcase, you and the students can take it and throw it in the dumpster!

LIVE IT

LIVE IT (5-10 minutes)

Ask: With the passage from Matthew 5 in mind, how does Jesus want us to respond to those we call our enemies?
Answer: Love them and pray for them.

Help the students understand that this is not an easy command from Jesus. Culture tells us to strike back, but Jesus says to love and pray for them.

Say: If there was anyone that had a reason to seek vengeance, it was Jesus. He was beaten and mocked by the soldiers and the political and religious leaders before his crucifixion. As he hung on the cross, he was wearing a crown of thorns and had a sign above his head that said "King of the Jews"—all as a mockery of him. The soldiers were gambling for his clothes. What a humiliating way to die. As the Son of God, Jesus had great power. He could have easily come off the cross and killed everyone around him. What did Jesus do instead? He said "Father, forgive them; for they do not know what they are doing."(Luke 23:34, NRSV)

Ask: With Jesus' teachings in mind, what are some positive things we can do instead of seek vengeance?

DISCUSSION QUESTIONS

Give each student a piece of paper and a pen or pencil. Have them write down ways they can love their enemies instead of taking vengeance on them.

Write down answers on newsprint or a dry erase board for all to see.

Help the students realize that there are many ways to make a positive influence on our culture which is filled with violence, pain, and suffering.

Examples: If you lost a loved one to cancer, take out that anger and pain by participating in a cancer walk. If you have been bullied, join a cause to stop bullying. If you are upset by hunger and poverty, help in a soup kitchen, food bank, or homeless shelter. If you see other students who are hurting, become a friend to them. If someone is mean or rude to you, don't get angry; show kindness to them.

Say: We may not have super powers like Superman or really cool gadgets like Batman, but God has equipped us with our own set of talents and abilities. We can use those talents and abilities to show love and kindness to each other, even to our enemies.

Close in a Prayer of your own or something similar to this prayer:

God, as we have read, it is not our responsibility to seek vengeance. Help us to follow Jesus' example and show kindness to those who hurt or wrong us. Amen

NOTES

Resources used in compiling background information: Comic Book Character by David Zimmerman, dictionary. com, Holy Superheroes by Greg Garrett, The Psychology of Superheroes edited by Robin Rosenberg, Romans by Paul Achtemeier. Pictures used: Batman by Wacko

DAREDEVIL AND DISCERNMENT
BY JIMMY BYRD AND ANDY McCLUNG

SCRIPTURE
1 KINGS 3: 5-12, JEREMIAH 29:13, 1 CORINTHIANS 12:10,
1 KINGS 19:11-13

THEME
Discernment requires discipline, and it's one of the most
important abilities we can develop.

CONNECTING TO YOUR STUDENTS

Your students are certainly aware of disabilities, and may even know someone with a disability. They're not likely, however, to know anyone who's completely blind; less than 1% of the U.S. population is seriously vision impaired, and few of them are completely blind.

It's possible your students who need corrective lenses have wondered what it'd be like to go blind. It's also possible your students don't know Daredevil. He has consistently appeared in various media since 1964, but has never been well known to the general public.

Discernment is nothing new to your students. They do it every day: "Which channel do I watch?" "Should I go out with this person?" Discernment about life-defining choices, however, may be unfamiliar territory. Good thing, too, because teens are just now developing the ability to understand the permanence of some decisions. It's not social maturity, but physiological. Their brains are just now developing that ability.

EXPLAINING THE TOPIC

Daredevil first appeared in Daredevil #1 in 1964, called "The Most Unusual Hero of All." Storm controls the weather; Daredevil reads by feeling the ink with his fingertips. Hulk crushes tanks; Daredevil identifies your deodorant from two blocks away. Flash runs faster than the speed of sound; Daredevil tastes every ingredient in a casserole. When Superman gets shot with a missile, it bounces off his chest; when Daredevil gets shot with a handgun, he bleeds freely and passes out. "Unusual" indeed. And... he's blind.

Matt Murdock was raised by his father, a washed-up boxer who made young Matt promise to live by using his brains, not his fists. Matt studied hard and never fought or played sports. Bullies taunted him calling him a daredevil.

In his teens, Matt saved a blind man from being hit by a truck. A canister of radioactive material fell from the swerving truck onto Matt's face. It blinded him, but also heightened his other senses to incredible levels. When his father was later killed by a crooked fight promoter, Matt put on a mask, took the name the bullies had taunted him with, and used his heightened senses to bring the killer to justice. He continued to fight for justice—in the courtroom as an attorney and on the streets as a superhero.

Imagine daily life as Matt. You hear every cell phone, every radio and TV, every voice, cough, sniff, and foot-step for 500 yards. You smell what everybody around you has eaten today, which laundry detergent they use, their pets, and which deodorant they're wearing. You feel the air moving around people, cars, and buildings. You taste the pollutants in the air. You're completely in touch with everything around you. How do you sort through all these distractions and focus on what's important?
By using discernment.

For Daredevil, discernment is distinguishing between the sensory impressions that constantly bombard him so he can determine priorities. For us, it's the spiritual practice of assessing and evaluating a situation to determine what God wants so that we can make decisions undistracted by temptations or self-delusions. Solomon knew the importance of discernment. In 1 Kings 3:5-12, he could have asked God for anything, but he asked for wisdom to discern.

Daredevil's origin was later expanded to show Matt almost going crazy from the hyper-sensory input, but then learning to develop discernment through discipline.

Matt decided he wanted to control his hyper-senses instead of retreating from the noisy world. We must want to discern God's voice amid all the distractions of this world. To find God we have to seek God with our whole heart (Jeremiah 29:13). That's not easy. We'd rather keep certain parts of our hearts away from God.

Matt learned to sort through all those distractions and pay attention to what's important. We deal with plenty of distractions, but we already know how to pay attention to the things we care about, to hear what we love above the distractions. But do we care enough about God to pay attention to God?

Daredevil knows his city. Matt Murdock knows the courtroom. He has mastered both worlds. The more familiar with God we are, the more likely we are to discern God's call. We know those with whom we spend time, like when close friends say the same thing at the same time. We come to know God by spending time with God. Part of that must be listening in silence. We can't expect God to break through our spiritual busy-ness.

Matt works in the courtroom and Daredevil works on the streets, taking two different approaches toward the same goal: justice. This shows us that there can be more than one right way to fulfill God's call. A call to feed the hungry can be answered by sending money to Heifer International and by working in a soup kitchen. When Daredevil hears a mugging four blocks away, he doesn't stay where he is. He goes to the rescue. Discernment is pointless if we're not willing to take action on what we hear from God.
Daredevil's nickname, "The Man without Fear" goes along with the whole image, like a circus daredevil fearlessly performing death-defying feats. He jumps off buildings, swings from a cable, and stands up to bad guys far more powerful than him. To answer God's call, we must step forward without fearing failure, what others think of us, or doing something new.

Many stories show Daredevil reflecting on his actions, wondering if he's done the right thing, feeling guilty for those he hurt and those he couldn't help. After we take action based on discerning God's call we need to reflect, assessing what we did and how we did it, asking ourselves how well we did what God called us to do.

THEOLOGICAL UNDERPINNINGS

According to our Confession of Faith, God speaks to humankind through the Bible, natural and historic events, and persons (1.02). We know from experience, though, that we can't always easily hear God. Because being a Christian is about far more than saying the right words or believing the right thing to ensure you go to heaven after you die, each and every Christian must use discernment to hear God calling him or her to embrace a specific vocation, to engage in particular ministries, to pursue distinct topics of study. We also need discernment to hear God calling us to worship and service, but these two things are much easier to "hear" because they become habitual. The truth is, even if we're doing them regularly, it may be out of habit rather than answering God's call.

All believers need the ability to discern. Paul calls discernment a spiritual gift (1 Corinthians 12:10), meaning that God has given this ability to some believers; they only need to discover it within themselves. The rest of us need to develop it. This only happens through discipline, as described above.

Though this lesson is about discernment, it mentions justice. "Justice" is a term used a lot in our society. Many Christians discern God calling them to work toward justice. It's important to keep in mind that there are different definitions for the word "justice." The secular definition, especially in superhero stories, is "judgment of persons by judicial process" and/or "the administering of deserved punishment or reward." In other words: the bad guys getting the punishment they deserve. Justice for Christians, however, is something else entirely: doing what is right, or "just" in God's eyes. Applying the Lesson to Your Own Life

Which type of justice are you most drawn to: the courtroom kind, the kind a vigilante distributes in a dark alley, or the kind described as what's right in God's eyes? Which do you work toward, and how? Matt Murdock promised his father he'd use his brains instead of his fists. He keeps this promise by being a lawyer and only fighting when he's dressed as Daredevil, so it's Daredevil, not Matt, doing the fighting. Is this really keeping that promise? How have you rationalized breaking a promise? Have you ever experienced/witnessed a parent on a noisy playground hear his or her child's cry above the cacophony of other sounds? That's proof we already know how to pay attention to the things we care about, to hear what we love above all the distractions in our world. What keeps you from hearing God? Or, put another way: What do you love so much that its call drowns out God's call?

JUST IN CASE

If a student seems interested in the character of Daredevil, you might mention that among superheroes, he is one of the few shown to be religious. He is a Roman Catholic, sometimes shown in church or consulting a priest. His mother, whom he thought had died long ago, actually left home to become a nun. This is refreshing in an entertainment medium that usually ignores religion, and when it does pay attention, often portrays Christians as either crazy, clueless to the real world, or hypocritical.

DAREDEVIL AND DISCERNMENT
BY JIMMY BYRD AND ANDY McCLUNG

SCRIPTURE
1 KINGS 3: 5-12, JEREMIAH 29:13, 1 CORINTHIANS 12:10,
1 KINGS 19:11-13

LEADER PREP

RESOURCE LIST
- Blind folds

- Children's puzzles containing around 10 pieces

- Newsprint or dry erase board

- Paper and pencils/pens for each student

- TV, DVD, CD player, radio, fan, etc. to make noise

BEFORE LESSON
Make sure you have several different devices for making noise: a TV, DVD, CD player, radio, fan, etc. Be as creative as you wish for the noise making in the section LISTEN UP. You will also need to make copies of the 1 Kings 3:5-12 handout for each student.

GET STARTED

GET STARTED
OPTION 1: This idea is influenced from a game on an episode of CBS's Survivor. Have each student get a partner. Give each pair a puzzle that has already been disassembled. One student will be blindfolded and will have to work the puzzle using only the verbal directions of his/her partner of where the pieces should go. The kicker is that all the students will be working on the puzzles at the same time. Not only will the blindfolded kids have to listen to know where the puzzle pieces go, they will have to specifically listen for their partner's voice over all the other voices.

If you have enough time you may give each partner a turn at solving the puzzle.

Ask: Was it frustrating trying to work the puzzle with so many voices giving out orders at the same time?

Sometimes it can be frustrating trying to maneuver through our culture with so many voices telling us to do this and do that. As Christians we have to listen for God's voice in all of the noise that is around us.

DISCUSSION QUESTIONS

OPTION 2: Have one student maneuver through some basic obstacles to get from one side of the room to another side. Basic obstacles can be going around chairs, under tables, etc. The student must be blindfolded. Pick another student to be the GPS. This person must stand on the other side of the room and give directions. The other students will yell out misleading directions. The student that is blindfolded must listen to the voice that is his/her GPS. You can have the students take turns doing this.

Ask: Was it frustrating trying to move through the course with so many voices giving out directions at the same time?

Sometimes it can be frustrating trying to maneuver through our culture with so many voices telling us to do this and do that. As Christians we have to listen for God's voice in all of the noise that is around us.

DISCUSSION QUESTIONS

LISTEN UP

LISTEN UP (10-15 minutes)

Say: Daredevil is a superhero that relies heavily on his senses of hearing, touch, taste, and smell. Why not his vision? Daredevil is blind. Imagine being Daredevil about to take on a room full of bad guys, and he can't see a single one of them. The only way he knows how to get to them is with his other heightened senses. Daredevil must use discernment to take out the bad guys.

As always, feel free to read the description provided for each superhero at the beginning of the lesson.

Say: While you were blindfolded for the activity, you got a glimpse of what it is like for Daredevil to have to discern which sounds to listen to in every situation.

Say: We must use discernment every day to help us to make right decisions and to listen for God's voice in the "noise" of our world.

Say: Do you all realize how much "noise" we have in our lives everyday?

"Noise" can be anything that is a daily distraction.
Examples: music, cell phones, TV, Facebook, Twitter, etc.

On a piece of newsprint or dry erase board, have the students list all the different "noises" they face every day.

Say: With so much noise in our lives, is it any wonder why we have a hard time listening to God's voice for direction?

At this time tell the students you are going to read 1 Kings 19:11-13. The Message
As you read the scripture, make sure that there is a lot of "noise" in the background. Have loud music playing, a TV or DVD playing, tell students they can play on their phones or tablets, etc. As all of this noise is going on, read the scripture in a soft voice. Read the scripture several times; each time you read it, take away one of the distractions until it is just you reading the scripture.

"Then he was told, "Go, stand on the mountain at attention before GOD. GOD will pass by." A hurricane wind ripped through the mountains and shattered the rocks before GOD, but GOD wasn't to be found in the wind; after the wind an earthquake, but GOD wasn't in the earthquake; and after the earthquake fire, but GOD wasn't in the fire; and after the fire a gentle and quiet whisper. When Elijah heard the quiet voice, he muffled his face with his great cloak, went to the mouth of the cave, and stood there.

NOW WHAT

NOW WHAT? (10 minutes)
Have someone read 1 Kings 3: 5-12.

Go over the Developing Daredevil's Discernment handout with your class.

Have the students write down at least two ways they will try to pay attention to God more on a daily basis. Have them share their answers with the rest of the group. If a student finds this to be too personal, then please do not push them to share.

Every year at church camp we had this thing called Quiet Time. Each evening after worship, everyone spread out and sat quietly. This would last about 10 minutes, giving everyone a chance to talk to God, listen to God, or to simply be still and listen to the world around them. Year after year, many of the campers said Quiet Time was their favorite part of camp. It helped them to realize how often they didn't stop to do that.

LIVE IT

LIVE IT (5 minutes)

Challenge the students this week to go without one of their "noises." Maybe go without Facebook, Twitter, or Instagram for the week. Maybe no music for the week or no TV. For most, this will be very hard to do.

I did this one with my youth group. We went without music for one week. I was amazed at how much music I normally listened to. It was very hard for me not to instinctively turn on the radio every time I got into my car.

The purpose of this exercise is to help the students develop some discipline when it comes to discernment. Every time they go to turn on the radio, TV, computer, etc., they replace that time with listening and talking to God. Instead of TV, pray; instead of music, read the Bible or a devotional book; instead of the computer, do something active like serving.

Close in prayer or through a Quiet Time.

DEVELOPING DAREDEVIL'S DISCERNMENT
1 Kings 3:5-12

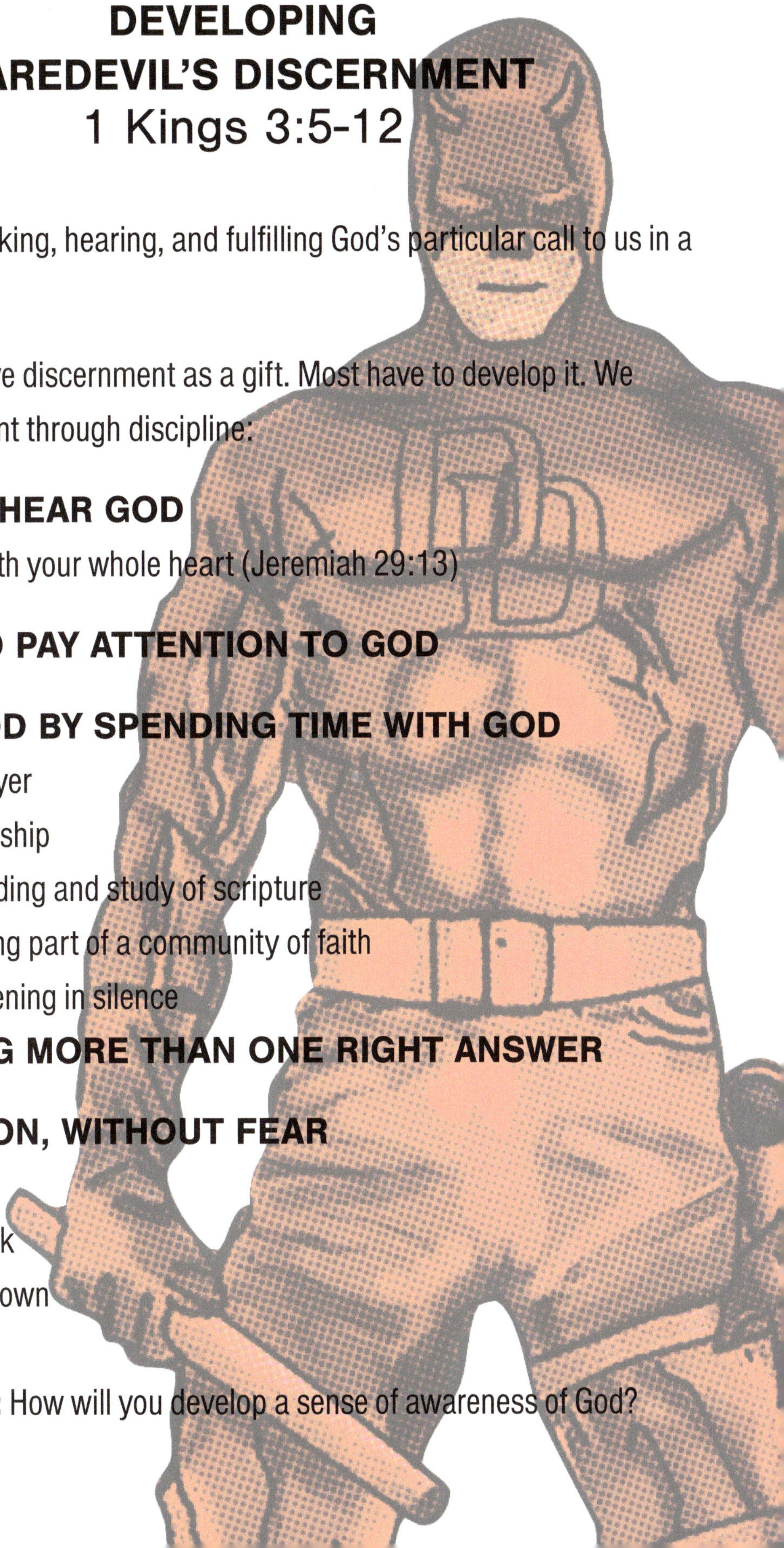

Discernment is seeking, hearing, and fulfilling God's particular call to us in a given situation.

A few believers have discernment as a gift. Most have to develop it. We develop discernment through discipline:

WANTING TO HEAR GOD

Seek God with your whole heart (Jeremiah 29:13)

LEARNING TO PAY ATTENTION TO GOD

KNOWING GOD BY SPENDING TIME WITH GOD

Through prayer

Through worship

Through reading and study of scripture

Through being part of a community of faith

Through listening in silence

RECOGNIZING MORE THAN ONE RIGHT ANSWER

TAKING ACTION, WITHOUT FEAR

Of failure

Of what others think

Of the new or unknown

REFLECTION: How will you develop a sense of awareness of God?

NOTES

Resources used in compiling background information: dictionary.com, nfb.org, "Touch the Future" training materials produced by the CP Church, Westminster Dictionary of Theological Terms, Who Needs a Superhero? by Michael Brewer. Pictures used: "Deardevil" graphic created by FitraSantos with edits and comicbook action - http://goo.gl/pivR1J, "Road Sign" by Taber Andrew Bain with text changed to "This Way, That Way" with edits and comicbook actions - https://goo.gl/87wlHc, Hermon Hamfest PA "Speakers 3D" by Acadia3D with edits and comicbook actions, "Hilton Key Largo Resort signpost" by Matt Kieffer with edits of sign text and comicbook actions - https://goo.gl/iPLPrC

FAITH OUT LOUD

THE MASQUERADE PARTY
BY JIMMY BYRD AND ANDY McCLUNG

SCRIPTURE
MATTHEW 22:34-40; MATTHEW 7:21, MATTHEW 25:31-36

THEME
Christians don't look different than anybody else, but they should be easy to spot by their behavior.

CONNECTING TO YOUR STUDENTS
Teens know about concealing identity.

Online anonymity affects many. Something about not having to look at another person and seeing the effects of our words causes us to say cruel things we would never say in real life. Almost 60% of kids have had cruel things said to them online, nearly 43% have been bullied, and 81% agree such things are easier to do online than in person.

Teens "try on" different social roles to figure out and declare who they are. Teens' changing looks are their way of trying to find where they belong, where they fit in.

Some teens put on the mask/costume of not caring what others think of them when they really do, or acting as if everything is okay when it's not.

Some church-going teens wear the costume of well-behaved Christians, at church and at home, when that's not really who they are. Or, they may love Jesus and strive to be good, but conceal this to better fit in and avoid embarrassment when with their peers.

EXPLAINING THE TOPIC
Most superheroes wear masks and costumes. Let's consider three reasons for this.
First is a practical reason within the real world. Different artists may not draw the same character in exactly the same way, and different actors portraying one character certainly don't look alike. But when they put that character in a costume, readers and viewers know exactly who it is. The costume identifies the character. Plus, those costumes look dramatic. They draw the eye to comic book covers or movie posters and generate sales. (Most people in the real world, though, would want something more protective than spandex when going up against a gang of armed thugs, and would probably get into all sorts of problems when wearing a long cape!)

Second is a practical reason within the fictional world. It's easier to run, move, fight, and swing from cables in spandex than in regular clothes. Some costumes, like Captain America's, are a statement in themselves. Some costumes, like Batman's, are designed to strike fear into bad guys. Moon Knight uses his cape like a glider. Iron Man's armor is his costume; it's where all his defenses and weapons are. Batman's belt holds all sorts of helpful devices. In a 1986 story, Batman confesses that he has that bright yellow oval on the chest of his otherwise dark costume because it draws the eye, and aim, of criminals, and that's where his body armor is strongest.

Third is to keep secret identities secret. Superheroes know that without concealing their identities, their enemies might hurt their loved ones. A standard element in superhero stories is that the hero keeps his or her crime-fighting escapades secret from even those closest to him or her. An equally standard element, though, is that the heroes interact with friends and family in both their identities. And somehow, the people closest to them never catch on to who they really are. Standup comedians have made fun of this for years. Why wouldn't Lois Lane realize that Superman looks just like Clark Kent without his glasses? Would Robin's tiny little mask really conceal his identity? The image of a superhero, though, is more than just his or her face. The first episode of Lois & Clark: The New Adventures of Superman (1993) addressed this by showing Clark Kent and his adoptive mother, Martha, trying several possible costumes for Clark to wear as Superman. When Martha declared the winner (the flowing red cape, the bright S-motif on the chest, the blue tights that reveal every muscle), Clark wonders aloud about the lack of a mask. Martha replies that no one is going to be looking at his face.

So, while tiny little masks or the lack of glasses wouldn't really fool anybody for long, superhero stories aren't supposed to be overly realistic. It's interesting, though, that secret identities seem to be playing less and less of a role in many storylines. Many characters (She-Hulk, Iron Man, Thor, Daredevil, Captain America, Hank Pym, Luke Cage, Wonder Woman) have either dropped using a secret identity or have had their identities revealed. As superhero characters have been adapted for TV and movies in recent years, the costumes have been made less cartoonish. What works in a small panel on a small page doesn't always work on a giant movie screen. Compare Christopher Reeve's costume from 1978's Superman to Henry Cavill's from 2013's Man of Steel. Compare the X-Men costumes from the comic books to those in the movies. (There is an in-joke about this in the X-Men movie from 2000. When Wolverine makes fun of the black leather costumes, Cyclops says, "Would you prefer yellow spandex?" Wolverine wore yellow spandex in the comic books.)

Most superheroes wear unique and easily identified costumes. Some people in the real world do that too. It's easy to know some people's occupations just from how they're dressed: nurses, police officers, fire fighters, auto mechanics, chefs. It's easy to know what some people like just from how they're dressed: a Black Cadillacs tee-shirt, a St. Louis Cardinals cap, a New York Knicks jersey. It's even easy to know some people's religion just by how they dress: a priest or nun, Hassidic Jews, Mennonite, Amish, a Buddhist monk, a Muslim. (Some of these examples aren't necessarily religions but are, at least, sets of beliefs.)

So how would someone spot a Christian just by looking? Crosses worn as jewelry won't do it, because lots of people wear a cross more as a fashion statement than a theological statement; worse, many people consider them some kind of good luck charm or see no significance in them at all. Christians, as a whole, don't dress in a specific way that broadcasts their faith. But there is a way to spot Christians just by looking: by their behavior.

THEOLOGICAL UNDERPINNINGS

Some people who claim to be Christians, either blatantly or by implication, are only pretending. They may be active in church, know the Bible, and even do works of service. But if they have not fully given control of their lives to God through Jesus Christ, they're not Christian. We're not talking about believers who sometimes sin. Every believer does (Confession of Faith 4.23). We're not talking about people on their way to becoming Christians. We're talking about people who think or claim that they are Christians, but aren't. Such people may be fooling themselves and others, but they're not fooling God.

Jesus said not everybody who calls him Lord will enter heaven (Matthew 7:21). Jesus talked about two groups calling him Lord, but only one enters heaven (Matthew 25:31-36). The dividing factor in both these passages is their belief in Jesus as Lord being lived out in their actions. When asked which was the greatest commandment, Jesus said nothing about belief or appearance, only behavior (Matthew 22:34-40). When James defines "pure and undefiled" religion, he mentions only behaviors (James 1:27).

Becoming a Christian is based on belief: we cannot save ourselves, and so must rely on Jesus Christ. It's also based on behavior: repenting of sin, accepting forgiveness through Jesus, and determining to serve both God and other people (Confession of Faith 4.08). Far too often, all the emphasis is put on the believing and repenting part, with little or no emphasis on the service part.

What we believe affects what we do. You believe that a stove is hot, so you don't touch it. You believe in gravity, so you don't jump off roofs. You believe your spouse is faithful, so you don't panic when they're a little late getting home. You believe Jesus Christ was God incarnate, died, and was resurrected to save the world from sin and death, so you serve God and others.

God was incarnate in Jesus 2,000 years ago. He preached, taught, healed, comforted the hurting, and confronted evil. Today, we Christians, the Church, the Body of Christ, are supposed to do all of those things as well. Paul calls this clothing ourselves in Christ (Galatians 3:27). So it's not the clothes, but the behaviors we "wear" that show Christ within us. And just to be clear: doing good things isn't what saves us; we do good works because we are saved (Confession of Faith 6.08).

Did you dress up for Halloween as a child? If so, what were some of your favorite costumes? Why those? Was there a costume you always envied but never got to wear?

How many "masks" or "costumes" (social roles) did you "try on" as a teen? Which role, looking back, is most embarrassing? Which one fit the best? Did you stick with it?

If you were to become a superhero, would you wear a bright attention-getting costume, something that would protect you, something very practical, or would you try to create something that does all of the above? Do you have to dress a certain way for your occupation? If so, would a total stranger know your occupation just by seeing you dressed for it? If not, would you prefer that you did have to dress a certain way?

If someone who knew nothing about you were to observe you, secretly, from Monday morning to Saturday night, when do you think they would figure out that you're a Christian?

APPLYING THE LESSON TO YOUR OWN LIFE
Did you dress up for Halloween as a child? If so, what were some of your favorite costumes? Why those? Was there a costume you always envied but never got to wear?

How many "masks" or "costumes" (social roles) did you "try on" as a teen? Which role, looking back, is most embarrassing? Which one fit the best? Did you stick with it?

If you were to become a superhero, would you wear a bright attention-getting costume, something that would protect you, something very practical, or would you try to create something that does all of the above? Do you have to dress a certain way for your occupation? If so, would a total stranger know your occupation just by seeing you dressed for it? If not, would you prefer that you did have to dress a certain way?

If someone who knew nothing about you were to observe you, secretly, from Monday morning to Saturday night, when do you think they would figure out that you're a Christian?

THE MASQUERADE PARTY

BY JIMMY BYRD AND ANDY McCLUNG

SCRIPTURE
1 KINGS 3: 5-12, JEREMIAH 29:13, 1 CORINTHIANS 12:10,
1 KINGS 19:11-13

LEADER PREP

RESOURCE LIST

- Construction paper
- Markers
- Stickers
- Crayons
- Tape

- Yarn or string
- Pencils or pens
- "Welcome to the Masquerade" lyrics
- "Do I Have A Secret Identity?" worksheet
- Lyrics to "We Are One in the Spirit"

- You will need the song "Welcome to the Masquerade," by Thousand Foot Crutch. It can be found on CD, iTunes, or Google Play.

GET STARTED

GET STARTED (10-15 minutes)

OPTION #1: Give everyone some construction paper, markers, stickers, etc. Have them make and decorate their own superhero mask. Use string or yarn to keep the masks on their faces. After everyone is finished, have them put on their masks for everyone in the class to see.

OPTION #2: Do a superhero fashion show. Have the kids bring a store bought or homemade costume with them to class. Let everyone get dressed up and have a fashion show to show off all the different costumes.

LISTEN UP

LISTEN UP (15-20 minutes)

Dressing up can be fun. Whether we are dressing up in a costume for Halloween, a play, or for a party, it can be fun to pretend we are someone else. Cos-play and LARPing are big trends today.

LARP stands for Live Action Role Play. Driving through Nashville one day, I saw a bunch of people dressed in medieval attire having a mock battle—a form of LARPing.

Say: Most superheroes wear masks and costumes to conceal their identity. They do not want people to know who they really are. This keeps the bad guys from interfering in their personal lives. Peter Parker is a newspaper photographer in his personal life; he puts on a costume and becomes Spiderman in his super hero life. Matt Murdock is a lawyer in his personal life; he puts on a costume and becomes Daredevil in his superhero life. Clark Kent works as a reporter for a newspaper in his personal life, but saves the world as Superman in his superhero life. As you can see, these people are living double lives.

Ask: Do you ever feel like you are living a double life? Do you ever feel like you are pretending to be someone you are not?

Say: With the internet, it has become easier to live a double life. People can set up fake profiles and be someone else online. People can spend a lot of their time playing in online gaming communities, living out adventures. There is even an online community called Second Life where you can live out a virtual life.

"Virtual Reality (VR), which can be referred to as immersive multimedia or computer-simulated life, replicates an environment that simulates physical presence in places in the real world or imagined worlds. Virtual reality can recreate sensory experiences, which include virtual taste, sight, smell, sound, and touch." (Wikipedia.)

Ask: Is it healthy for people to live a double life?

Ask: Where do you draw the line between reality and virtual reality?

Ask: When it comes to your Christian faith, do you find yourselves living a double life?

Allow time for discussion. Then pass out the sheet entitled "Do I Have A Secret Identity?" to each student. Give them time to fill it out, and then discuss the answers.

Play the song "Welcome to the Masquerade," by the band Thousand Foot Crutch. You can also give each student a copy of the lyrics on the handout found at the end of the lesson. After listening to the song, ask the students their interpretations of it.

One interpretation of the song is that it is about being afraid to share your faith. Another is that the world is a masquerade ball, and we should take off our mask and just be ourselves.

NOW WHAT? (10 minutes)

Ask: So how do we drop the mask and be the person that Jesus has called us to be?

On newsprint or dry erase board, write down all the ways that the students come up with to let others know they are followers of Christ.

After the answers have been recorded, sing the song "We Are One in the Spirit." The students may be familiar with the song from church camp or church worship service. There is a handout with lyrics at the end of the lesson. The key to the song is the line, "They will know we are Christians by our love."

NOW WHAT

Have someone go back and read Matthew 22:34-40 again.

Ask: What is the most important way we can let others know we are Christians?
Answer: Love

LIVE (5-10 minutes)

Wearing a mask or costume can give us a temporary escape from reality. That's the thing—it's not reality, it is pretend. Reality is still there when the mask comes off. Will we be made fun of because of who we are? It's very probable. They hated Jesus.

LIVE IT

Have the class work together to write a prayer. This prayer will be to help hold each other accountable to just be themselves—the person whom Christ has called them to be.

NOTES

Resources used in compiling background information: "11 Facts About Cyberbullying" by dosomething.org, Comic Book Character by David Zimmerman, imdb.com. Pictures used: "Mask" by Vassilis with edits and comicbook actions, "Can not hide" by B Tony with edits and comicbook actions https://goo.gl/4XkMeO, Mask Rack by Rog01 with edits and comicbook actions - https://goo.gl/JiIajL, "Detail - Masks (Nigeria)" by Andrew Moore with edits and comicbook actions - https://goo.gl/u6gZWE

"WELCOME TO THE MASQUERADE"
BY: THOUSAND FOOT CRUTCH
LYRICS BY: STEVE AUGUSTINE, TREVOR MCNEVAN, AND JOEL BRUYERE
FROM THE ALBUM: WELCOME TO THE MASQUERADE

WE'VE GOT THE FIRE, WHO'S GOT THE MATCHES?
TAKE A LOOK AROUND AT THE SEA OF MASKS
AND COME ONE, COME ALL
WELCOME TO THE GRAND BALL
WHERE THE STRONG RUN FOR COVER
AND THE WEAK STAND TALL

I'M NOT ONE TO SCATTER ASHES
BUT THERE'S SOME THINGS THAT'LL MELT THE PLASTIC
TRY AND DIG DOWN DEEPER IF YOU CAN

I'M NOT AFRAID, I'M NOT ASHAMED, I'M NOT TO BLAME
WELCOME TO THE MASQUERADE
I'M NOT ASHAMED, I'M NOT AFRAID, I'M NOT O.K.
WELCOME TO THE MASQUERADE
WELCOME TO THE MASQUERADE

WE'VE GOT THE POWER
WHO'S GOT THE ACTION?
BREAK IT DOWN, 'TILL THERE'S NOTHIN'
BUT A MERE FRACTION
OUT OF THE FIRE, RISE FROM THE ASHES
REJECT YOUR DOUBT, AND RELEASE THE PASSION

LET'S GET ON IT
BELIEVE, IF YOU WANT IT
STEP INTO THE REALM
WHERE THE REAL ONE'S FLAUNT IT
COME, BACK, REWIND
ANOTHER TIME ON IT
REACH OUT, TAKE THAT
ONE OFF, STEP ON IT

WE ARE ONE IN THE SPIRIT

VERSE ONE
WE ARE ONE IN THE SPIRIT,
WE ARE ONE IN THE LORD.
WE ARE ONE IN THE SPIRIT,
WE ARE ONE IN THE LORD.
AND WE PRAY THAT ALL UNITY MAY ONE DAY BE RESTORED.

AND THEY'LL KNOW WE ARE CHRISTIANS BY OUR LOVE,
BY OUR LOVE,
YES THEY'LL KNOW WE ARE CHRISTIANS BY OUR LOVE.

VERSE TWO
WE WILL WORK WITH EACH OTHER,
WE WILL WORK SIDE BY SIDE.
WE WILL WORK WITH EACH OTHER,
WE WILL WORK SIDE BY SIDE.
AND WE'LL GUARD EACH MAN'S DIGNITY
AND SAVE EACH MAN'S PRIDE.

VERSE THREE
WE WILL WORK WITH EACH OTHER,
WE WILL WORK SIDE BY SIDE.
WE WILL WORK WITH EACH OTHER,
WE WILL WORK SIDE BY SIDE.
AND WE'LL GUARD EACH MAN'S DIGNITY
AND SAVE EACH MAN'S PRIDE.

VERSE FOUR
WE WILL WALK WITH EACH OTHER,
WE WILL WALK HAND IN HAND.
WE WILL WALK WITH EACH OTHER,
WE WILL WALK HAND IN HAND.
AND TOGETHER WE'LL SPREAD THE NEWS
THAT GOD IS IN OUR LAND.

DO I HAVE A SECRET IDENTITY?

When it comes to being a Christian, I find it _____ to be myself at:

HOME:	HARDEST	1	2	3	4	5	EASIEST
SCHOOL:	HARDEST	1	2	3	4	5	EASIEST
WORK:	HARDEST	1	2	3	4	5	EASIEST
A PARTY:	HARDEST	1	2	3	4	5	EASIEST
A BALLGAME:	HARDEST	1	2	3	4	5	EASIEST
CHURCH:	HARDEST	1	2	3	4	5	EASIEST
A CONCERT:	HARDEST	1	2	3	4	5	EASIEST
CHURCH CAMP:	HARDEST	1	2	3	4	5	EASIEST

As Christians, why do we feel the need to be one way with a person or group and another way with a different person or group? Why can't we just be our Christian selves all the time?

Read these following scriptures: Matthew 7:21, Matthew 25: 31-36, and Matthew 22: 34-40.

What do these scriptures from the Gospel of Matthew say about living your Christian faith?

WONDER WOMAN AND THE TRUTH
BY JIMMY BYRD AND ANDY McCLUNG

SCRIPTURE
JOHN 8:32, JOHN 14:16, JOHN 18: 33-38, 1 JOHN 1:8-9

THEME
Truth is bigger than our feelings and more important than we think.

CONNECTING TO YOUR STUDENTS

Your movie-loving students may be aware that Wonder Woman is supposed to appear in some upcoming movies. Your comic book readers may know her. Although she's consistently been around since 1941, your other students may only have heard of her.

Your students may think there is nothing, outside of math and (maybe) science, that's unequivocally true. This may shock you, or you may be right there with them; it depends on your age. The last few generations have grown up in a world that gives equal value to all opinions, and harshly criticizes anyone who doesn't. An opinion doesn't even have to be an informed opinion to have value. "Is that true?" is considered archaic. Now it's, "Is that true for me? Is that true in this situation?"

Truth is important. Salvation through Christ is not an opinion, provable scientific fact, or a solvable math problem. But it is truth—an eternally important truth.

EXPLAINING THE TOPIC

Wonder Woman wasn't the first female superhero, but she was the first to achieve popularity and longevity. She first appeared in All-Star Comics #8 in 1941. At the time, women in comic books were rarely anything more than love interests or damsels in distress for the male heroes to woo or save. Wonder Woman broke this mold. She is extremely strong, resistant to damage, can fly (originally in an invisible jet but later on her own), and a skilled warrior. She wears bracelets with which she can deflect bullets in flight. Plus, she carries a magic and unbreakable golden lasso.

In the days when most superheroes were created by young men, Wonder Woman was created by William Moulton Marston, a middle-aged psychologist and women's rights activist, at the request of a publisher who wanted to quiet the criticism that comic books were too violent. Marston pitched Wonder Woman as a character based on love, beauty, and truth rather than masculine violence. He believed a strong female character would both attract female readers and show them that they could do anything. Those early years of Wonder Woman, though, sent mixed messages. Sure Wonder Woman was strong, capable, and independent, but she also ran around in a skimpy costume and was frequently tied up by men. The skimpy clothes might have been to keep male readers interested, but Marston said the bondage scenes were only to show Wonder Woman later escaping—literally from the ropes or chains, and metaphorically from the bonds of male-imposed gender roles. People are still debating if Marston was more feminist or fetishist.

Her origin story says Wonder Woman doesn't fit the mold of the stereotypical 1940s American woman because she was raised in an all-female society in which all roles— leaders, warriors, nurturers—are filled by women. She comes to our civilization to return a male soldier who crash-landed on this secret island home and to share their superior values with us. She is introduced with: "At last, in a world torn by the hatreds and wars of men, appears a woman to whom the problems and feats of men are mere child's play." Early stories show Wonder Woman, disguised as Diana Prince, confused by our world with all its war, hatred, crime, and tension between genders.

Some superheroines are just copies of male characters (She-Hulk, Batgirl, Supergirl), but Wonder Woman is mostly original. Marston did draw from Greek myths about a race of fierce warrior women called Amazons. Female supervillains were already around (Batman's foes Catwoman and Poison Ivy), but when Wonder Woman's archenemy Cheetah was introduced in 1943, readers saw two super-powered women fighting for the first time.

Wonder Woman's lasso is particularly interesting. When around someone, it forces them to tell the truth. Marston would go on to invent what eventually became the polygraph, or lie detector. (Marston's device only measured blood pressure. Polygraphs measure multiple physiological reactions.)

Truth is powerful. Step 1 in twelve-step programs is to recognize the truth: "We admitted we were powerless over alcohol—that our lives had become unmanageable." Until an addict, anorexic, bulimic, or abuser recognizes and admits the truth, there can be no healing. This is why confession has long been a part of Christianity. As long as we maintain the lie that we're not sinful, we can't be forgiven (1 John 1:8-9). A comic story in 2000 revealed that Wonder Woman regularly uses her lasso to reveal any lies she's telling herself so she can stop. She knows she can't fully be who she's supposed to be with self-deception in her life.

Lies, or untruthfulness, breed more lies. Unfaithful spouses, upon being caught, often express relief because managing a web of lies is so stressful. Telling the truth is much easier.

Nowadays many people consider truth to be subjective. What's true for you might not be true for me; what's true in one situation might not be true in another. Thus, nothing is absolutely true. Stepping onto a lake, however, ends up with somebody getting wet, no matter how strongly they believe they can walk on water. Someone with the opinion that the grumpy lion at the zoo just needs a hug will need a lot of stitches and several units of blood. In a 2002 story, Wonder Woman's Lasso of Truth is broken in battle, resulting in all truth dissolving. Whatever people believe becomes truth: the moon is made of cheese, 2 + 1 = 4. This story affirms the ridiculousness of thinking our opinions or beliefs shape truth. Instead of thinking that, we're better served to allow truth to shape our opinions and beliefs.

Mike Brewer highlights the saddest aspect of subjective truth: "If the only truth is my own beliefs, then I will never find a truth bigger than myself." He also says, "Truth can set us free, but opinions cannot."

THEOLOGICAL UNDERPINNINGS
Some people confuse truth with fact. Facts are indeed true, but truth is bigger, more spiritual, than mere facts. If you brag about taking second place in a foot race but don't mention there were only two runners, you've spoken fact, but not truth. The statement "God is good" is true, but can't be proven as factual. That it's the opinion of millions of people isn't what makes it true.

God created men and women "equal and complementary" (Confession of Faith 1.11), designing each gender to need the other. As much as some try to say there's no difference between men and women,

the truth is there are some things each gender is generally better at doing. People who deny this, blame culture for limiting gender expectations into children, but even atheists recognize specific gender roles in humankind. For example: men became hunters because, on average, they can throw a spear harder and farther than women and wouldn't have to leave the hunt to deliver or nurse babies.

We cannot save ourselves. As much as we'd like that to be false, it's true. Cumberland Presbyterianism was partially born by breaking away from strict Calvinism, which says we have no say in our salvation. CPs didn't go so far as say it's completely up to us whether or not to accept salvation, though. We believe God calls us to salvation and gives us the faith to respond to that call, but it's still our own free will choice.

Before Pilate, Jesus said he was born and came into this world to testify to the truth, adding, "Everyone who belongs to the truth listens to my voice." When Pilate asked, "What is truth?" Jesus didn't respond. He'd already told his disciples, "I am the way, and the truth, and the life". (John 18:33-38, 14:6)

APPLYING THE LESSON TO YOUR OWN LIFE

Plenty of movies and live-action TV shows have featured male superheroes. To date, Wonder Woman has appeared in only one live-action TV series (1975-1979), and no movies. There have, however, been several failed TV pilots and movie attempts. Why do you think it's been so hard for Hollywood to bring Wonder Woman to the screen?

Do you think men and women could do everything equally well if, from childhood, both genders were equally taught domestic and nurturing skills, how to emote, and physical assertiveness, or are there inborn differences between the two genders that significantly affect behavior?

If Wonder Woman lassoed you, what question would you most fear she might ask?
Do you believe some things are true, regardless of what anybody thinks about them or what can be proven? If so, what are some of those things? If not, then how do you define truth, and what did Jesus mean by calling himself "the truth"?

DIGGING DEEPER

Lots of research shows that, on average, men and women are far more alike than different in personality, psychology, cognitive ability, and sexuality. Where they differ in these areas, they differ by small margins. Those small margins, however, sure seem to cause a lot of conflict. Differences in grip strength and running speed are only slightly greater. Where men and women differ significantly, on average, is muscle mass and strength. Perhaps because this difference is so universal, there are fewer conflicts over it.

WONDER WOMAN AND THE TRUTH

BY JIMMY BYRD AND **ANDY McCLUNG**

SCRIPTURE
JOHN 8:32, JOHN 14:16, JOHN 18: 33-38, 1 JOHN 1:8-9

LEADER PREP

RESOURCES
- 2 pieces of paper for each student

- Pencils or pens

- A hula hoop

- Newsprint or dry erase board and markers.

GET STARTED

GET STARTED (10 minutes)
Have each student write down on a piece of paper two things about themselves that are true and one thing that is false. After everyone is finished, pick one person to read their three statements. The rest of the group must figure out which one is a false statement. Give everyone a chance to read their three statements.

Ask: How easy or hard was it to deceive each other with your one false statement?

LISTEN UP

LISTEN UP (20 minutes)
Say: Today we are learning about truth. Chances are, since you were a little kid, you have been told to always tell the truth.

What if there was a magical device that when it touched you, it made you tell the truth no matter what?

Say: Wonder Woman is a superhero from DC Comics and also a member of the Justice League. She has many special powers including: super strength, ability to fly, incredible combat skills, and resistance to harm.

There is a complete background on Wonder Woman at the beginning of this lesson by Andy McClung. You may want to share in more detail about Wonder Woman to those who are not as familiar with her.

Say: One really cool thing that Wonder Woman has is a golden lasso that when wrapped around someone, makes them tell the truth.

Place a hula hoop on the floor. (A yellow or golden hula hoop would be perfect!)
Ask for a volunteer to stand in the hula hoop. Explain that when standing in the hula hoop, they will be asked 5 questions, and they have to tell the truth.

First set of questions for volunteer
1) Have you ever fallen asleep in church?
2) Have you ever cheated on a test at school?
3) Have you ever disobeyed your parents?
4) Have you ever peed in a public pool?
5) Are you a One Direction fan?

Second set of questions for another volunteer
1) Have you ever thrown up on a fair ride?
2) Have you ever had a crush on Justin Bieber?
3) Do you believe in ghosts?
4) Have you ever sneaked out of your house?
5) Have you ever stolen anything?

Ask: Was it hard to tell the truth? These were fairly easy questions to answer truthfully, but what if it had been very personal questions to answer, and the hula hoop really was a magical device that made you tell the truth?

Ask: Why is telling the truth so important?

Say: Now here is a deep question: What is truth?
(Your class may have various answers on what they think truth is; make sure and listen to each one.)

DISCUSSION QUESTIONS

Say: Let's look at what the Bible says about what truth is, and then we will answer the question again: What is truth?

Have someone read John 8:32, another person read John 14:6, and another read John 18:33-38.

Say: After hearing these three passages read, can you tell me what truth is?

Write down answers on newsprint or a dry erase board. Give the class time to discuss their answers.

NOW WHAT

NOW WHAT? (10 minutes)
On the supernatural TV show "The X-Files," their slogan is "The Truth is Out There," which corresponds to the two main characters who are always looking for the truth in the midst of conspiracies and paranormal events.

OPTION 1: Give each student a piece of paper and something to write with. With the previous scriptures in mind, have them each write their own slogan about truth. After everyone has finished, have them share their slogan with the rest of the class.

OPTION 2: Have students draw or paint a slogan about truth. Let them be as creative as they want to be. When they are finished, have them show the rest of the class.

LIVE IT

LIVE IT (5 minutes)
Read 1 John 1:8-9 to the class. "If we say that we have no sin, we deceive ourselves, and the truth is not in us. If we confess our sins, he who is faithful and just will forgive us our sins and cleanse us from all unrighteousness."

Say: We are obviously not perfect, and we will make mistakes and not always tell the truth. Does that mean that God loves us less? (No!)

Close with prayer, giving your students time to pray silently and confess any lies they may have told; Close with this declaration of pardon:

"The mercy of the Lord is from everlasting to everlasting.
I declare to you, in the name of Jesus Christ, you are forgiven.
May the God of mercy, who forgives you all your sins,
Strengthen you in all goodness, and by the power of the Holy Spirit keep you in eternal life." Amen.

(The Service for the Lord's Day – Supplemental Liturgical Resource 1 - Pg. 53 – 1984 Westminster Press)

NOTES

Resources used in compiling background information: Alcoholics Anonymous 4th ed., Comic Book Character by David Zimmerman, comics.org, dccomics.com, dictionary.com, imdb.com, npr.org, The Psychology of Superheroes edited by Robin Rosenberg, "Understanding the Mysteries of Human Behavior" by Mark Leary, Who Needs a Superhero? by Michael Brewer. Pictures used: "1978 Superman & Friends Greeting Cards" by Mark Anderson with edits of comicbook actions - https://goo.gl/g12LDb, "Speak the truth, even if your voice shakes" –Maggie Kuhn Cringle Park, Levenshulme, Manchester" by Duncan Hull with edits and comicbook actions - https://goo.gl/PmLkYN, "Lie & Truth Sign" by geralt with edits of comicbook actions - https://goo.gl/Mk9hz2, "Lwp Kommunikáció" by Próbára tett profik (Alexis Conran) with edits of comicbook actions - https://goo.gl/JVFvSI

FAITH OUT LOUD

SUPERMAN
BY JIMMY BYRD AND ANDY McCLUNG

SCRIPTURE
JOHN 3:16, 1 PETER 2:21, LUKE 19:1-10, LUKE 23:32-35,

THEME
Superman can be a picture of Jesus. So can we.

CONNECTING TO YOUR STUDENTS

Some teens may like Superman. Some may think he's just for little kids. But everybody knows about Superman because of his proliferation in every media: radio, movies, TV, novels, comic books, music, newspapers, YouTube, video games, and even a Broadway musical. Plus, his image—or at least his stylized "S"—has been seen on almost every consumer product imaginable, even human flesh (as tattoos). Everybody either knows Superman or at least knows about him.

Everybody knows about Jesus too. He has also shown up in most media, and he plays a feature role in the best selling book of all time. But knowing about Jesus and knowing Jesus are very different things.

Church-going teens may connect with Superman and Jesus as living in two "worlds" at the same time. Superman is a powerful being from another planet, but also Clark Kent. Jesus was fully human yet fully divine. Your students live in a very secular world, while also trying to live a very different life of faith.

EXPLAINING THE TOPIC

Mike Brewer, a pastor in Kentucky, tells about a time he wore a lapel pin of Superman's "S" symbol to church. It generated a lot of jokes about leaping tall steeples. But one woman seemed offended. She asked if the "S" stood for "savior," or for "Son of God." When Mike said it didn't, she grew irritated and asked, "Then what does it mean?" Mike answered, "The 'S' stands for Superman." This woman clearly thought something so frivolous didn't belong in church, so he added, "And Superman stands for Jesus."

Many stories have explored this connection, which is surprising considering Superman's history. In the 1930s, two Jewish teenagers, Jerry Siegel and Joe Shuster, created Superman. They made several weeks' worth of comic strips and tried to sell them to every newspaper they could contact, but nobody bought them. The boys edited their work into a comic book and convinced Detective Comics to publish it. Nobody expected it to sell well. Back then comic books were primarily newspaper comic strips, collected and reprinted in magazine form. (This is why we call them "comic books," even when they're not comedic.) The only original stories in comic books at the time were science fiction, spy, or crime stories. The latter included a few masked crime fighters called "mystery men", but none had super powers.

Superman debuted in Action Comics #1 in June of 1938, and sold 200,000 copies. By issue #7, half a million copies were selling every month, which means that 1 out of every 260 people in the U.S. was buying a copy.

Here's Superman's story: The planet Krypton has a very advanced culture. One man, Jor-El, knows Krypton is dying and wants to save everybody, but no one will listen to him. All he can do is put his infant son, Kal-El, in an experimental rocket and send him to Earth just before Krypton explodes. Kal-El lands in Smallville, Kansas, where he's adopted by the Kents. They name him Clark, love him as their own, and when they discover that our yellow sun gives him extraordinary abilities, they teach him to use these special powers for the common good.

Back in 1938, nobody knew we'd still be talking about Superman today or that a copy of Action Comics #1 would sell for $3,207,852 in late 2014. Over the years, details have been added to the origin story. Now we know Jor-El knew his son would have super powers here on Earth so he recorded messages instructing Kal-El to use his powers to help the people of Earth and to keep his identity secret, because if we humans knew who he really was and what he was capable of, we would fear, reject, and kill him, even though he came to help us.

Whether those two Jewish boys meant to or not, they made Superman have a lot in common with Jesus. They were both sent by a loving father to a world in desperate need of help. They both arrived miraculously—one in a rocket ship (outlandish in 1938), and one being born to a virgin (still outlandish today). Great danger surrounded both their arrivals—a planet exploding with one, and a slaughter of innocent babies with the other. Both were raised by good-hearted, working class parents who knew the child wasn't really theirs, but belonged to the world; their job was to prepare him for the mission only he could fulfill. Both grew up in small towns and went to the big city as adults—one to Metropolis and one to Jerusalem. They both became famous for doing incredible things to help people in need. In his first adventure, Superman stopped the execution of an innocent prisoner, saved an abused wife, and kept a corrupt politician from starting a war for financial gain. Throughout the gospels, we see Jesus work toward similar issues of justice. The similarities go on and on.

Anybody who thinks about Superman or Jesus long enough will wonder, "If he's really so powerful and so good, why doesn't he just take over the world and get rid of all the bad stuff?" To answer this, a 1998 story had Superman deciding to end world hunger. He flew all over the world carrying trucks, freight cars, and flatbeds full of food. He was welcomed in many places, but in one country starving people rioted and fought over the food. Somewhere else a crowd of hungry people threw rocks at him, suspicious of his motives. One dictator seized the food for his own profit. One government, knowing that hungry people are easier to control, fired a missile at him when he arrived with a ship full of grain. Superman wasn't hurt, the grain was destroyed, and the people remained hungry and oppressed. The story ends with Superman realizing that he can't save us from things like hunger, and war, and poverty, and disease...because as long as people are able to make choices, those evils will still be around.

THEOLOGICAL UNDERPINNINGS
Superman and Jesus both know their roles are servants, not dictators. Jesus could feed 5,000,000 as easily as 5,000, heal all diseases as easily as he healed ten lepers, call down 10,000 angels to stop oppression and end all war. But he knows those evils will still be around as long as people are able to make choices, and he knows God will always allow us to make choices.

Superman can put out forest fires, but can't prevent the carelessness that starts them. Superman could find a cure for cancer on some distant planet, but can't make us stop polluting our environment and bodies with carcinogens. Superman could use his X-ray vision to find more oil, but can't keep us from using more than we need. Superman can stop individual crimes, but not the poverty and injustice and oppression and greed and addictions that cause so much crime. Superman can do lots of things, but he can't change what's in our hearts that leads to so much of the world's misery. Superman can't, but Jesus can. And Jesus wants to. And Jesus will when we surrender our lives to him.

In many stories Superman makes himself vulnerable for the sake of humankind. Jesus was Almighty God, made vulnerable by choosing to become human in order to save humankind.

Both Jesus and Superman live in two worlds. Kal-El is just as much meek and un-athletic Clark Kent as he is Superman; Jesus was both fully divine and fully human. Had Kal-El's rocket landed in Russia (as explored in a 2003 story), or New York City rather than Kansas, Clark would have been very different. Had Jesus been born to a rich, powerful woman, Jesus would have been very different. Neither difference would have been conducive to their respective missions.

Superman and Jesus do have a lot in common. But only Jesus is real. Superman may even stand for Jesus, as Mike Brewer said, but it's more important for us to ask whether or not we stand for Jesus.

APPLYING THE LESSON TO YOUR OWN LIFE
What's your earliest memory of Superman? How has your impression of him changed since then? What's your earliest memory of Jesus? How has your impression of him changed since then?

If you had to choose just one, which of Superman's super powers would you like to have? Why that one? How would you use it? If you had to choose just one way for others to see Jesus in you, what would you choose? Why that one? What's stopping you?

If you were writing a comic book story or a TV or movie script about Superman, would you put more emphasis on his weaknesses or his strengths? On his super powers or on his humanness? Why? As you think, talk, and teach about Jesus, do you put more emphasis on his divinity or his humanity? Why? Do you feel like you live in two "worlds" or try to balance two natures within yourself? If so, what helps with that?

JUST IN CASE

If a student mentions the 1992 storyline in which Superman dies at the hands of intergalactic villain Doomsday, but is then mysteriously resurrected in several different forms, praise the student for seeing the death and resurrection connection with Jesus. This storyline, however, was more of a marketing ploy than veiled theology, so don't try to go too far down that road.

SUPERMAN
BY JIMMY BYRD AND ANDY McCLUNG

SCRIPTURE
JOHN 3:16, 1 PETER 2:21, LUKE 19:1-10, LUKE 23:32-35,
JOHN 8:1-11, LUKE 22:47-53, MATTHEW 5:43-48

LEADER PREP

RESOURCE LIST
• Man of Steel movie clip

• Newsprint or dry erase board

• Markers

• Colored pencils or crayons

BEFORE THE LESSON
Make sure to cue up the video. The clip starts at 44:17. The clip ends at 48:56. It can be a DVD or on Netflix or another streaming video.

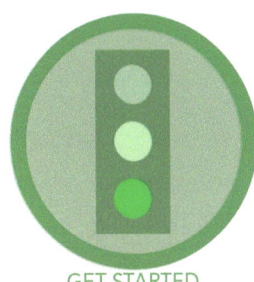

GET STARTED

GET STARTED (10 minutes)
Have each student draw their own Superman symbol with their own initial in it. Have them draw the first letter of their first or last name where the "S" would normally go. When everyone is finished, have them show them off to the rest of the class. Their personal super symbols will be used for the closing Live section. If you have a student who is artistic and can draw the symbol outline for the others, that would be great too!

LISTEN UP

LISTEN UP (20 minutes)
Say: Today we are going to be talking about two people who are great role models—one not real—Superman, and one who is real—Jesus.

Say: Superman is one of the most famous and recognizable superheroes worldwide. He has pure motives; he does not act out of vengeance like Batman or Punisher. Superman simply uses the powers he has been given to do good and help others. Superman seems to genuinely care for the people of Earth.

A background on Superman is included at the beginning of this lesson, if you want to share it with the students.

Show the clip from the movie "Man of Steel." The clip starts at 44:17 and ends at 48:56. If you are unable to find the movie clip, there is a summary of the clip on the website: http://www.thesource4ym.com. Simply click on Free Resources and Ideas, click on Movie Clip Discussions and then look for "Man of Steel."

Have the class write down on newsprint or dry erase board reasons why Superman makes a good role model.

Next, have the class divide into pairs, and assign each pair one of these scriptures: Luke 19:1-10, Luke 23:32-35, John 8:1-11, Luke 22:47-53, John 3:16, and Matthew 5:43-48.

After they have read the passages, have each pair tell how their passage shows Jesus being a role model. Record the answers on newsprint or dry erase board.

Now compare the two: Superman and Jesus.

Say: Both came to earth to save humanity, both stand for truth and justice, and both are great role models. Only one is real (Jesus), and only one can truly save us (Jesus).

Say: Both Superman and Jesus are great role models, but you know who else is supposed to be a role model? We are! As Christians, we are to be a living example of our faith in Jesus Christ.

NOW WHAT

NOW WHAT? (10-15 minutes)
Read 1 Peter 2:21-25:
"*This is the kind of life you've been invited into, the kind of life Christ lived. He suffered everything that came his way so you would know that it could be done, and also know how to do it, step-by-step.*

He never did one thing wrong,
Not once said anything amiss.

They called him every name in the book, and he said nothing back. He suffered in silence, content to let God set things right. He used his servant body to carry our sins to the Cross so we could be rid of sin, free to live the right way. His wounds became your healing. You were lost sheep with no idea who you were or where you were going. Now you're named and kept for good by the Shepherd of your souls."

This passage talks about the example of Christ and how we, too, must be a living example. Have the class act out this scenario:

Role play scenario #1:
Someone from school, whom you have a deep grudge against, shows up at your church for either Sunday school, youth group, or worship.

Ask: What do you do? How do you treat that person? How can you be an example of Jesus' love to that person?

Say: Church is a place where everyone should feel accepted and loved, whether it's Sunday school, youth group, worship, etc. No one should ever attend a church and feel rejected. Unfortunately, too many people have been hurt by "church people."

DISCUSSION QUESTIONS

Role play scenario #2:
You are about to take a big test at school, and you are worried because you haven't studied enough for it. Your best friend has already taken the test and has written down the answers. He or she gives you a copy of the answers—by taking this you are guaranteed to ace the test.

Ask: What do you do? Are you being a good example if you use the answers to cheat on the test?

DISCUSSION QUESTIONS

LIVE IT (5 minutes)

Have everyone look at their personal Superman symbol from the opening activity.

Say: Let this symbol remind you to try your best to be a living example or role model of the love of Jesus. No one can actually be a "Super Christian"; we are not perfect, but we should try our best. We are to simply be a follower of Jesus and love others the way that Jesus would.

Close in prayer.

NOTES

Resources used in compiling background information: census.gov, usatoday.com, The Psychology of Superheroes edited by Robin Rosenberg, Who Needs a Superhero? By H. Michael Brewer. Pictures used: "Superman statue" by Joseph Novak with edits and comicbook actions - https://goo.gl/w46FDx, "Superman" by Nicholas Rumas - https://goo.gl/4Dh1PX, "Head of Jesus Christ 11" by Waiting For The Word with edits and comicbook actions - https://goo.gl/DcXFru, "Student at Shree Dharmasthali Lower Secondary School, Pokhara, Nepal." by Department of Foreign Affairs and Trades Photostream - https://goo.gl/DJStHt.

FAITH OUT LOUD

SUPERHERO TEAMS IN THE COMICS AND THE CHURCH
BY JIMMY BYRD AND ANDY McCLUNG

SCRIPTURE
1 CORINTHIANS 12:12-27, 1 PETER 4:8-10, ROMANS 12:2,
PHILIPPIANS 3:2 JOHN 8:1-11, LUKE 22:47-53, MATTHEW 5:43-48

THEME
Each congregation is a team and a community with
particular members, benefits, challenges, and goals.

Connecting to Your Students

Teens know the value of being on a team (athletics, band, academic teams) and want to belong somewhere. It's built in to them. It's why they so readily adopt school rivalries, or an "us vs them" tension with adults or between cliques. Teens, like everyone else, desire true community. They want to belong. Some teens who don't find community in a family turn to street gangs—a twisted sense of family, but a clearly defined community to be a part of. Peer groups serve the same purpose, only generally more healthily.

Whether or not they have the vocabulary to express it, teens know a poorly functioning community when they see it, such as sports team with an abusive coach or a church congregation unsure of what it's supposed to be doing or how it's supposed to be doing it. They're not attracted to such communities.

Teens know what it's like to feel unappreciated, their gifts being unused. They know what it's like to feel out of place, as if they don't belong anywhere in the whole world.

With Spirit-led attention, superhero teams can speak to these needs.

Explaining the Topic

It didn't take long for comic book publishers to guess that if people liked reading about the adventures of individual superheroes, they'd probably love to see a group of superheroes having adventures together. In regards to storytelling, a team of superheroes can take on more powerful bad guys—or even whole armies—than a lone superhero can. Plus, readers get to see a different side of individual characters as they interact with peers instead of just fighting villains.

Let's consider what we can learn from super teams.

The Justice League of America first appeared in 1960. The team includes DC Comics' most popular characters, plus a rotating cast of lesser known characters. Initially, stories revolved around simply getting the job done. The team would come together, stop the mega-threat, and then go their separate ways. Readers got to see the heroes interact, but only superficially. DC's writers eventually learned from Marvel and began to explore the relationships of the characters to one another and together as a community. Leadership experts say any group (a committee, the church session, a sports team) has two purposes: first, get done whatever they came together to do, and second, take care of its members. A team that only gets the job done can't fully rejoice in their success, learn from their failures, or grow as persons. A team that only focuses on taking care of each other will never get the job done.

The Fantastic Four debuted in "Fantastic Four #1" in 1961, and broke many comic book stereotypes. They were a family first, before becoming superheroes. Reed and Sue were dating, Johnny was Sue's brother, and Ben was Reed's best friend. They bickered with each other, something unheard of among superheroes. They didn't wear masks or have secret identities...or even wear costumes until readers demanded it. A key member was a woman. Readers saw the first teenage superhero who wasn't just a sidekick, the first black superhero (Black Panther, introduced in 1966), the first superhero wedding, and the first time superheroes became parents. Plus, instead of just beating up villains, this team often outsmarted them and many times even showed them compassion.

The Fantastic Four teach us what it means to be a church family. They help each other grow personally and professionally. When they disagree, they still love and support each other. Within this family, timid Sue gained the confidence to change her name from the Invisible Girl to the Invisible Woman. Within this family, Reed, who agonized over his failures, finds forgiveness and learns to forgive himself. Johnny, the hot-headed loner, that when he gets knocked out of the sky, a member of this family will be there to catch him. When pessimistic Ben, hideously transformed, repulses people by his appearance or his temper, it's this family who assures him that he's loved. Many stories involve outsiders wanting to become part of this family, and they're always welcomed. These are all things a church family should do as well.

Marvel Comics brought together their top heroes in 1963 with "The Avenger #1." This team began with more character depth than the Justice League, as members argued among themselves. The director of "The Avengers" (2012) drew on those early stories, saying, "These people shouldn't be in the same room, let alone on the same team." Many stories feature characters being less argumentative after working together to defeat the villain. In a 1964 story, the Avengers discover and rescue a frozen Captain America. Being a natural leader, he soon becomes their leader and trainer. In later stories, Cap insists leadership rotate on a monthly basis. Membership on his team has been quite diverse: aliens, supernatural beings, mutants, androids, sentient robots, humans with technology-based powers, humans with biology-based powers, skilled humans with no powers, and even former supervillains who became heroes because of the Avengers. The Avengers teach us several important lessons about team membership. Team members don't all have to agree to get the job done; conflicting personalities can lead to different approaches to a common goal and thus increase chances of success. Most people naturally fit into some role within the team. A good leader isn't jealous of others' skills but strives to build up those skills. Shared leadership keeps one person's vision from directing the team's work; vision should be communal. A good team is diverse in abilities and personalities; a whole team of people with similar skills and approaches has fewer paths to success. An effective and successful team draws others to it, even former opponents.

The X-Men first appeared in "X-Men #1" in 1963, billed as "The strangest super-heroes of all." They're mutants, born with such strange abilities or appearances that they don't fit in to society. Many mutants experienced persecution before finding the X-Men, and the storyline includes government persecution. They feel as if they don't really belong in this world. The Bible says the same thing about Christians. We're citizens of heaven, living on earth for now.

Theological Underpinnings
God created humans to be in community. In the first account of creation, "God created humankind in his image...male and female he created them. God blessed them, and God said to them, "Be fruitful and multiply, and fill the earth." (Genesis 1:27-28 NRSV) Notice how God created them, an immediate community. Also note that God's first commandment to humankind was to create more humans, to expand the community. Even in the second account of the creation, in which God makes an individual first, it wasn't long before "God said, 'It is not good that the man should be alone...'"(Genesis 2:18 NRSV) and made a companion for the man. Giving the man a companion wasn't just about sexual reproduction, but about community; none of the animals were a suitable enough companion because the man had power over them. He needed a peer, an equal.

Super teams are communities. So are congregations, Sunday school classes, youth groups, church committees, and church sessions. These communities need to be a diverse group working toward the same goal (1 Corinthians 12:12-27), just like the Justice League or the Avengers. The Cumberland Presbyterian Church recognizes this by very intentionally having leadership and authority shared between elders and clergy at every level of church government. These communities need to be full of people willing to love each other (1 Peter 4:8-10) like the Fantastic Four. Like the X-Men, these communities need to recognize and be focused on the truth that while they may exist and function in this world, they truly belong to another world (Romans 12:2, Philippians 3:2).

Applying the Lesson to Your Own Life
Have you ever been around other people, but still felt very alone? Compare that feeling to how you feel surrounded by people you know, love, and trust. How would a total stranger feel coming into your classroom or your church's sanctuary? Would it change things if the stranger didn't look like anybody else there?

What teams/groups were you a part of as a teen? How did being part of that community affect you? What teams/groups are you a part of today? How does being part of those communities help you? What benefit do you bring to those communities? Do these communities have a good balance of getting the job done and taking care of each other?

Does your class make decisions as a team, or does one person decide and everyone else must agree or be left out? Consider finding out how your congregation's session makes decisions. Does one person dominate or is everyone's vision considered important?

JUST IN CASE

If a student asks, the first superhero team was The Justice Society of America, first appearing in 1940, in "All Star Comics #3." The idea of a super team was still so new and the writers were still so unsure of its attraction, this first story consisted of a group of superheroes simply having dinner together, with each taking a turn to tell about one of his or her own, individual adventures. The story concluded, however, with the team being asked to come to Washington D.C. for their first adventure together in the next issue.

SUPERHERO TEAMS IN THE COMICS AND THE CHURCH

BY JIMMY BYRD AND ANDY McCLUNG

SCRIPTURE
1 CORINTHIANS 12:12-27, 1 PETER 4:8-10, ROMANS 12:2, PHILIPPIANS 3:2 JOHN 8:1-11, LUKE 22:47-53, MATTHEW 5:43-48 JOHN 8:1-11, LUKE 22:47-53, MATTHEW 5:43-48

LEADER PREP

Resources
• "Avengers" movie clip

• Newsprint

• Markers

• Pens/pencils

• Copies of the Spiritual Gifts Inventory from website
 (Found in the Listen Up section)

Before the Lesson
Make sure you cue up the scene from "The Avengers" movie; start and end times are listed in the lesson. If you don't own the movie, you can get it on Netflix, Red Box, or I bet at least one of your students owns the DVD. You will want to go to the website to print off copies of the Spiritual Gifts Inventory—one for each student.

GET STARTED

GET STARTED (10 minutes)
You are going to have your class spell out the word CHURCH, using only their bodies. They have to work together to form the letters. If you have a small class, you could have the students form one or two letters, take a picture, and then let them form the next letter or letters, taking a picture each time. If you have enough time, they could spell out the full name of your church.

LISTEN UP

LISTEN UP (20-25 minutes)
Say: Today we are going to talk about the importance of teamwork.

Ask: Can you name any superhero teams?
(Avengers, X-men, Justice League, Fantastic Four.)

Say: When superheroes group together to form a team they are even more powerful. Many times it takes that teamwork to be able to stop the bad guys. The Avengers are a great example of individual superheroes that came together as a team to defeat the bad guys, but gelling together as a team wasn't easy.

Show the clip from "The Avengers." Begin at 1:07:14, and end at 1:12:47.

Ask: What was wrong with the Avengers in this clip?

Ask: What happened when the Avengers began to work together as a team?

Say: The Avengers were able to defeat the bad guys because they functioned as a team, using each of their individual gifts and abilities to work together.

DISCUSSION QUESTIONS

You are a part of a team or group: Sunday school, youth group, church.
Read 1 Corinthians 12:12-27, and discuss the importance of each member of the body of Christ.

Say: You are a part of the body of Christ. What specific gifts and abilities do you bring to the group?

There is a spiritual gifts inventory on this website:
http://www.teensundayschool.com/122/activities/spiritual-gifts-analysis.php

Print a copy for each student and have them fill it out.
After everyone has finished, go over the scores with each student to help them figure out what their gifts are.
(This is just a basic spiritual gift inventory. There are much more comprehensive ones online or in books.)

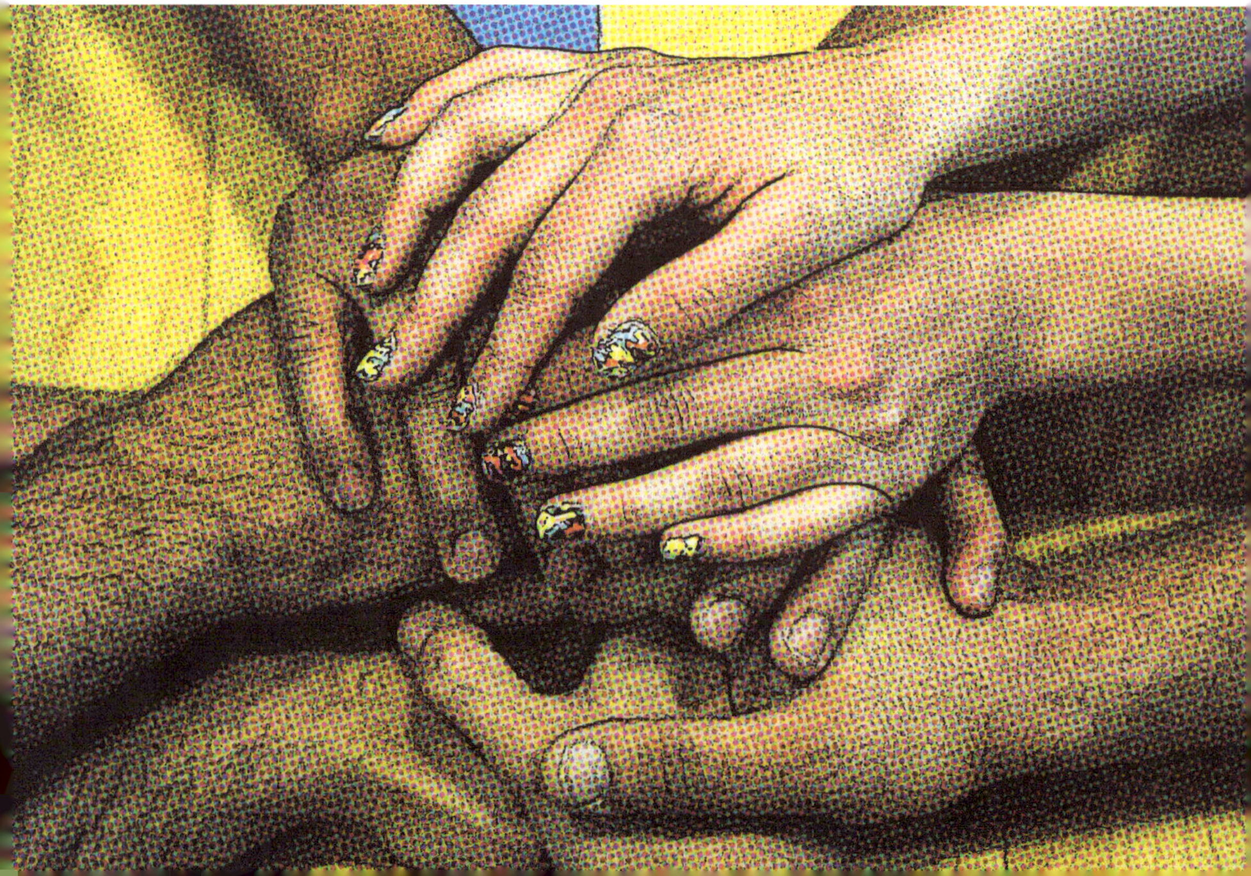

NOW WHAT

NOW WHAT? (10 minutes)

Say: Have you ever heard the statement that youth are the church of tomorrow? The reality is, you are the church of now! You can make a difference in your church right now.

On newsprint or a dry erase board, have the class name all the different committees and ministry teams in your church. Have the class talk about how they can be involved on those committees or teams as individuals or as a group, or any other ways they can be involved in the ministry of the church.

Ask: How can you use your talents and abilities to be involved outside the walls of the church—out in the community?

LIVE IT

LIVE IT (5 minutes)

Read the following passage from 1 Peter 4:8-10.

"*Most important of all, continue to show deep love for each other, for love covers a multitude of sins. Cheerfully share your home with those who need a meal or a place to stay. God has given each of you a gift from his great variety of spiritual gifts. Use them well to serve one another.*" (NLT)

Close in prayer, asking God to show each student which part of the body of Christ they are. Ask God to give each student courage and wisdom to be involved in the ministry of their church.

NOTES

Resources used in compiling background information: Comic Book Character by David Zimmerman, comics. org, imdb.com, Who Needs a Superhero? by Michael Brewer. Pictures used: "Dragon*Con 2013: JLA vs Avengers Shoot" by Pat Loika with edits of comicbook actions - https://goo.gl/64grKk, "Orlik Aerobatic Team 05" with edits and comicbook actions by Ronnie Macdonald - https://goo.gl/FDESgF, "2012 Warrior Games" by The U.S. Army - https://goo.gl/9QP8sU, "Dragon*Con 2013: JLA vs Avengers Gather" by Pat Loika with edits and comicbook actions - https://goo.gl/KTPcjW